The Broom Closet Collection
I

by

D. A. Lindsay

DORRANCE PUBLISHING CO., INC.
PITTSBURGH, PENNSYLVANIA 15222

Dedication

To my children: Maisha, Michelle, Merilyn, Bernard, and Marlena; who taught me many things while I was raising them.

ISBN-10: 0-8059-7056-8
ISBN-13: 978-0-8059-7056-2
Library of Congress Control Number: 2005932697

Printed in the United States of America

First Printing

For information or to order additional books, please write:
Dorrance Publishing Co., Inc.
701 Smithfield Street
Third Floor
Pittsburgh, Pennsylvania 15222
U.S.A.
1-800-788-7654
Or visit our website and online catalogue at www.dorrancebookstore.com

Contents

A Letter to an Absentee Father: Why, Daddy, Why?

Dear Dad:

Why, Daddy, why
did you leave me and Mom alone?
Why, Daddy, why
didn't you call me on the phone?

To tell me that I'm your princess,
that I'm Daddy's little girl,
an' that you wanted to protect me
from the whole wide world.

Why, Daddy, why
didn't you teach me not to be a fool,
how to choose a proper wife
and to follow the golden rule?

Why, Daddy, why
didn't you tell me it was wrong
to do anything to please the crowd,
sacrifice my honor to get along?

Why Daddy, why
wasn't I important enough to you
to remain a positive part of my life
and to help me make it through?

Daddy, did you think that
I wouldn't make you proud?
Well, you never taught me
not to curse and talk so loud.

Why, Daddy, why?
Why didn't you stay?

Why didn't you teach me about God
and teach me how to pray?

I'm so mad at you, Daddy.
I just wanna have a fit
because you don't love me.
I'm so mad that I could spit.

I'm so mad at you, Daddy!
Because you were never there
to show me that I'm important,
to show me that you care!

I'm so mad at you, Daddy!
My self-esteem is gone.
You never made me feel important,
so why should I carry on?

But Daddy, you know what?
I'm gonna do my life right.
Even though you weren't there for me,
for my future, I'm gonna fight.

You missed my first tooth
and my first day of school.
You missed teaching me to ride a bike.
To yourself, you were more than cruel.

You missed out on all the love
I had for you to give.
You know, you're real lucky, Pop,
that God continued to let you live.

Well, when I become a parent,
I'm gonna make sure that I'm there.
My child will *know* I love him.
My child will *know* I care.

I'll be there to see his first tooth.
I'll be there when he cries.
I'll be there to wipe the tears

from my precious child's eyes.

I'll teach my child to do right
and to do his best every day.
I'll teach him when the day is done
how to kneel down and pray.

So, Dad, this is the last time
I'll make the effort to stay in touch.
This letter is from your child
who could have loved you so, so much.

Sincerely,

Your Offspring

A Prayer: In the Midst of a Scream

They look at me and point.
They yell at me and say I'm crazy because
of my actions—But they just don't understand me.

They say I don't think ahead
and there's little to no sign of planning ahead in my life.
They *don't* understand me.

I live in a world of frightening yesterdays.
I live in a world of terrifying todays. And tomorrow is just too over-whelming to fathom.
They *don't* live where I live.

So, I don't plan ahead and just exist from moment to moment.
I'm afraid to fall in love with my life because at any moment it could be snatched away from me.
They *couldn't* live where I live.

I carry the anger of past hurts from a thousand generations,
and the walls of my prison collapse more and more each and every day.

I really wish I had the courage to break out of this prison, but there's no one outside to receive me if I get out. Everyone I really know is here with me.
They don't even want to *visit* me here.

I don't know when, but I'll die if I stay here and I'll die of loneliness if I leave. This not knowing when Death will come is driving me even more *insane.*

I both dread and embrace the thought of the end coming in unison.

I know this sounds totally insane to them, but perhaps You can help me.

I'm in the midst of a scream,
>a scream of pain,
>a scream of terror
>a scream of hopelessness

I can neither move forward
>or backwards
>or sideways.
The pain is too great.

As I scream with this all engulfing agony,
I can't hear them tell me which way to go.
I can't see them point to the right path.

And they are too frightened of me to love me and to allow me to feel their embrace.
>So please, I ask You, Lord Jesus,
Tell me in the voice that's loud enough from He who has ears to hear
>Where to go,
>What to do.

Please, I ask You, Lord Jesus,
>Show me how to open my spiritual eyes so that I may see the safe path You have provided for me to travel.

I've tried many paths at the counsel of a multitude of others, and still, I feel empty.

Please, Lord, take me in Your loving arms and teach my spirit to feel *peace*.

Amen

Alarm

When the rain and hail
are crashing all about,
when the billowing cloudbursts
cause the heavens to shout,

When the falling snow
turns the night into day,
and when the glaring sun awakens
and chases the moon away,

When the walls meant to protect you
begin to tumble down,
don't forget God.
You know, He's always around.

No matter what the problem
or how bad the plight,
remember to walk by faith
and not to walk by sight.

All the Trimmings

Babies are like plain hotdogs.
They need mustard, ketchup, and a bun.
Sure, you can still eat them plain,
but then they're not half as much fun.

Babies are like sweet sugar cookies.
And with milk, the taste can't be beat.
Sure, you can eat them alone,
but swallowing might be quite a feat.

Babies are like creamy ice cream.
They're great in a bowl or a cone.
But things can get real messy
when ice cream is ice cream alone.

So, if you want to have a baby,
make sure you have all the trim.
The love, the patience, the finances, and the time
and a supportive husband whose name could be Jim.

Because babies are so very special
and deserve the best of everything.
So please, plan thoroughly for these little ones
and the more happiness their arrival will bring.

And if you already have a baby,
then you know what tune I'm spinning.
So, just be sure your next little one
comes with all the trimmings.

Anxiety

I just can't believe it!
My life is such a mess.
Why was I ever born?
Will I ever get some rest?

Seems like no matter what I do,
nobody is satisfied.
It just doesn't seem to matter
how hard I really tried.

It's just one thing after another,
and the pace is picking up.
It won't be very long now
before there's too much in my cup.

At the brink of the breaking point
when I feel like I'll just break,
then a soothing calm envelopes me
and I hear a voice softly say,

"Tomorrow is another day.
Tomorrow is now on the way.
It you just hold on and try to smile,
tomorrow will be here in a little while."

Just keep holding on
and just keep on trying.
There's really no shame
just 'cause you feel like crying.

For each and every problem,
there is a solution
just waiting around
for the proper execution.

All you have to do
is try your very best.
Then, no apologies are needed,
and you'll pass any test.

So, don't you give up.
The future's not cast in stone.
Remember, I AM is with you
and you're *never alone*!

Baby Momma Drama

Whine, whine, whine.
Oh, stop your complaining!
Stop crying about how
you wish you could change things!

You didn't complain at all
when I let you hit it.
No, you were pleased
when I said you could git it.

So, I got pregnant,
and you *know* it's yours.
One hairdo and one manicure late,
and I gave you them drawers.

But really, whose fault is it
that I'm yo' baby momma?
I gave you what you wanted,
so cut out all that drama!

If you were so concerned
about what kind of mother I would be,
seems like you would have taken
a longer time to see

If I was the kind
to care if a diaper's dry,
or if I was the kind
to care if yo' baby cries.

If I was the kind
to care what you thought,
I got what I wanted
so you better just step off!

In one week of begging.
I let you have it for a while.
But I never told you
I'd be changing my lifestyle.

I'm a good-time party girl
and you should have taken heed.
You should have kept your pants up
and never given me your seed.

So, now you have to suffer
because I'm the one you chose.
And you can tell your baby
that his momma is a ho!

Black on Black Crime

If ever you have neglected your rest,
to bed too late, can't function at your best,
two A.M. movies for sleep there's not enough time,
YOU have been a victim of black on black crime.

If ever you have smoked a blunt or jack
because you were feeling a little out of whack
and filled your lungs with smoke, poisons, and grime,
then YOU, TOO have been a victim of black on black crime.

If ever you have drank to excess an alcoholic beverage
because you thought it would give you extra leverage,
but all you did was act crazy and whine,
then YOU were a victim of black on black crime.

If ever you were in school and received your assignment,
and your pen and your paper never reached the same alignment,
and you didn't do work while on don't-feel-like-it time,
Another sad case of black on black crime.

Things happen in life, sometimes bringing harm.
Some things we can prevent, sometimes we're forewarned.
But I don't know anything that's any more wicked
than when black on black crime is self-inflicted.

Can You Touch My Heart?

So, you have an interest in me.
You say I caught your eye.
Well, what exactly do you mean by that?
Oh, you want to be my guy.
(Oh, you want me to be your guy.)

So, you say loving me will be easy
because I look so doggone good.
But, do you know my favorite color?
Someone who loves me surely should.

Do you know why I raise one eyebrow?
Do you know what I dream of?
Do you know how to touch my spirit?
Do you even know how to define love?

Can you soothe my wounded heart
with the comfort of just your words?
Can a special look you save only for me
make my soul feel free as a bird?

Can the mere thought of your great love for me
touch the innermost regions of my heart?
Can you embrace me with your spirit
so that I long never for us to part?

Can you walk with me side by side
with our steps being like as one?
As we accomplish our dreams together,
as we walk towards the sun?

So, if you are willing to love me,
not lust, but love that is true,
then love me first without touching me
and I'll return the same love to you.

Chaos

Beautiful young people
in the prime of their lives,
eyes dull with pain
while they struggle to survive.

Whole family in tears
at a drug dealer's wake
still got rent to pay,
no longer can they count on Jake.

Drug addict waits
on the corner for the "man"
so for one more time
instead of stooping, he can stand.

A young girl is crying.
She's afraid to go home.
She's got to tell her momma
that she's been out there playing grown.

She believed him when he said
the words "I love you,"
but that's the line he always uses
whenever he wants to screw.

Little girl playing
in her own bedroom
when out of nowhere
is heard a big BOOM!

Momma's in tears.
She has her baby no longer.
People try to comfort her,
make her will to live stronger.

Crack baby crying
nonstop into the night,
while Momma prepares her fix
so again, she can take flight.

Politicians talking about
waging war on drugs,
closing homeless shelters,
and arresting more thugs.

Off with the cap
of some imported rare wine,
as a businessman deals
in some white-collar crime.

Some people even say
this is hell and there's no heaven,
but there's one truth that can't be ignored,
as sure as five plus two is seven.

For as long as babies laugh
and a little child can smile,
then dark clouds are still hiding
silver linings all the while.

And the Eternal One still beacons
us to come to Him to rest,
and no matter what anyone says,
He truly loves us best.

If only we would come to Him
and make Him our choice today,
He'll take away all our fears
and wipe all our tears away.

Choices

Choices, choices, choices.
What choices will you make for yourself?
Will you do this, or will you do that?
Will you do what's good for your health?

It is legal for you to smoke cigarettes
until your lungs turn black like smoke
and pop right out of your chest and back.
And you keep wondering why you choke?

It is legal for you to drink
until your liver is so alcohol-infested
that it jumps right out of your nose and mouth
because of all the liquor you've ingested.

Choices, choices, choices.
The choices you make for yourself
can either help you live or help you die.
Will you choose what's good for your health?

Drain People

Drain people, drain people,
on their way to drown,
seeing how many people
with them they can take down.

You know, misery loves company.
And that is no lie.
Even when they laugh,
they really want to cry.

Because really, they are sad.
Their self-esteem is having a serious reduction.
Hating themselves and everyone else,
as they move toward destruction.

So, be sure that in your garden
of friends, there is no weed,
and all those you consider your friends
are truly friends, indeed.

Friends

What is a friend?
A person close to you
who agrees on the surface
with everything you do?

Who tells you only things
that make you feel swell?
Never saying what they mean
like, "Fool, go straight to H—-l!"

Well, I want a friend who,
whether I like it or not,
will tell me that cold is cold
and will tell me that hot is hot.

What is a friend?
A friend is a person who
tells you the truth
about the things that you do.

He's Everything to Me

Oh, how gracious and merciful You have always been to me!
Because of Your loving kindness, I strive to be what You want me to be.

I can't say "thank you" enough, to show my deep appreciation
for all the times You never left me and kept me from self-inflicted damnation.

When I open my eyes each morning and see Your sun in the sky,
I feel warmly reassured in the knowledge that You remain close by my side.

And I know that whatever obstacles I encounter in this life,
no matter how high the mountain, no matter how much the strife,

That You will always protect me, as long as I remember to stand.
I will keep my eyes on You and obey your every command.

For You commanded me to give up some "stuff" I had: sadness, hopelessness, and hate,
and replace them with love, peace, joy, and victory, and a ticket through the Pearly Gates.

And with all the underserved blessings You've given me ever since I was a child,
if you never did one single thing more for me, I'd just lay down with a smile and die.

But, you promised You'd never leave me,
an' I know Your word is true.
For, *You* owe me nothing, and I owe You *everything*,
and I'll spend eternity with you.

Inconsiderate People

Don't you just hate it
when people mess with your stuff?
Didn't ask for your permission
and don't return it, sho' nuff?

Don't you just despise it
when people get in your face
and apologize when they find they're wrong,
after they get all over your case?

Don't you just want to scream
when people talk too loud?
If it's an "A and B conversation,"
then why is it drawing a crowd?

Inconsiderate people,
the world with them is infested.
I try hard to avoid them
so that I don't get arrested.

Inner Beauty

Beautiful, fabulous people,
all ages, colors, and shapes,
fresh clothes, manicured toes,
what a visual impression they make!

The jewels in their rings—
Oh, how brightly they shine!
How I wish this was a guarantee
that their spirits were of like kind.

But unfortunately, that's not the case.
For too often, it is true
that the outward visage of people you meet
of what's inside won't give a clue.

An extraordinary beauty with
hands so soft to touch
may be a vessel that holds
a spirit of loathing and such.

Behind the seemingly sweet smile
of one so handsome and so tall
may be one who wants nothing less
than to be the one to cause you to fall.

Ah, it would be wonderful if
people would all strive to be
as beautiful on the inside
as the part that we can see.

Because we are God's precious children,
an' beautiful He made us, each one.
But the choice to be beautiful on the inside
belongs totally to us alone.

It Ain't Yo' Fault

It ain't yo' fault that Bay-Bay's yo' momma's name,
and you act just like her; things you do are just the same.

It ain't yo' fault that yo' daddy you don't know.
That's because yo' momma, yo' momma is a ho.

It ain't yo' fault that you act like a jerk
cause yo' momma always treats you like a nasty piece of dirt.

It ain't yo' fault that your elders you disrespect
cause yo' momma's nasty mouth ha' that particular effect.

It ain't yo' fault that you have the manner of a pig
and you think you gotta make the others look small so you can feel big.

It ain't yo' fault that you dress like a ho
cause yo' momma never taught you that your body's not for show.

It ain't yo' fault that your pants are hangin' down
cause yo' daddy never taught you better cause he was nowhere to be found.

It ain't yo' fault that on weed you're always smacked.
Soon you'll be like yo' momma, soon you'll be addicted to crack.

It ain't yo' fault that you act nasty and mean
cause yo' momma had you when she was fifteen.

It ain't yo' fault that you've become a parent while still in school.
Like yo' momma, you're another link in that long chain of fools.

So, are you man enough, or woman enough
to honestly look at where you are?
Are you just another link in the chain,
or are you a future star?

Did you know that chains can be broken
by just one single link
that chooses not failure,
but to get his or her life back in sync?

You don't have to continue.
You know, you really can stop.
Stop the madness from spreading.
Make your life not be a flop.

Whose life is it, anyway?
Your life or your momma's?
It's up to you to write your own life story
and to cut out all of that drama.

It takes a really brave person
to honestly look at what's ahead
and place themselves on a path
that does not lead to dread.

It's Over

I really, really love you.
You know that I do.
So, how can you tell me,
tell me that we're through?

I gave you my all.
Trusted you with my heart.
As we two joined as one,
you said we'd never part.

I thought you really loved me.
I was so doggone sure of it.
My friends tried to tell me
that you were just a wad of spit.

But I just wouldn't listen.
I guess that other girl is your next.
You never really loved me.
You're just in love with having sex.

I pity your next victim
who believes all of your lies
because your love is limited only
to what is between her thighs.

Now, I truly regret
opening my heart and letting you in
because sex with you is not love,
sex with you is SIN!

Lies

You know, lies are like a bridge.
They won't carry you to the other side,
but to the middle of the volcano,
where the lava flows deep and wide.

You know, lies are like a long ladder
that, when pointed toward the sky,
can be climbed to the very top
and give the illusion that you can fly.

You know, lies are like a balloon—
Full of lots of hot air.
But when its solidity is tested,
there is really nothing there.

Even though lies have been tested
for hundreds upon hundreds of years,
they still cause utter confusion,
leading to anger, frustration, and tears.

Living for the Moment

If you only life for the moment,
then the moment is all you'll possess.
But moments will successively get better
because careful planning leads to success.

But if positive planning followed by actions
are not ingredients in your life recipe,
then you life's stew will be like weak chicken broth
and taste as bland as bland can be.

As the moments of your life continue
to pass through the hourglass like sand,
be sure not to remain idle too long
so opportunity doesn't slip through your hands.

Love Yourself

Without any sugar,
you can't make a cake.

Without real diamonds,
the ring is just a fake.

Without a melody,
you've just got a poem.

Without film in the camera,
there'll be no photographs to show 'em.

Without gasoline,
your car ain't your ride.

Without love for yourself,
who's gonna stand by your side?

Because before you reach two,
you've got to get past one.

The task of loving yourself
simply must be done.

Mud Pies

I remember when you were three and spent so much time making the perfect mud pie, and your clothes were all muddy and I didn't stop you because you seemed so focused on your goal.

Then, when you were finally satisfied that your creation was as perfect as any mud pie could possibly be, you took it out of your make-believe oven and triumphantly brought it for me to see.

I remember hiding the look of dismay that wanted to creep upon my face because the cute little sunsuit you were wearing (the one with the little hearts on it, my favorite) was covered with mud and looked like it would never, ever be the same.

But the exuberant look of sheer glee on your face let me know that at that moment, the great desire burning within you was for me to be as proud, pleased, and exhilarated with your perfectly made mud pie as you were.

So I "oohed" and "ahhed" and looked at your creation in awe and wonder and gave you the biggest hug that let you know beyond the shadow of a doubt that all your toil and effort with the mid pie made me feel oh, so proud to be the mother of the wonder child who was the author of this perfect creation.

Now, years later, as I remember all those mud pies, I am often filled with that same burning desire that after I do my very best on a project and present my mud pies to my children, they would make me feel like I was their super mommy, the former wonder child, and the present author of some of the things that make them happy.

My Friend

I called out my friend's name,
but there was no reply,
I looked everywhere for her,
as I let out a heavy sigh.

I thought she was just hiding,
but I couldn't have been more wrong.
I searched for hints of her whereabouts
in the melody of the wind's song.

I asked all who knew her,
"Where could she possibly be?
I just saw her a little while ago.
Seems like she was just talking with me."

As I fell asleep that night,
she came into my dream
with bright lights all around her,
brighter than I'd ever seen.

The look on her face was pure joy,
and she did not speak a word.
And I noticed angel wings behind her,
then she flew high like a bird.

When I woke up, I realized
that I had found my friend.
But I would never see her face again
until I reach *my* mortal life's end.

My True Love

I want to find the one.
The one who will fall in love with me in the same manner in which I will love him.

My love is deeper than any ocean on any planet.
Falling in love with me is like gently free-falling into a bottomless chasm, where everything is always warm and fuzzy and you never have to worry about smashing into the bottom abruptly or even waking up hastily from a wonderful dream.

My love is taller than any mountain in the entire universe.
And the person I love will never desire to use outside stimulants: alcohol, marijuana, cocaine, or other women to feel high.

My love has no negative side-effects.

As I said before. I want to find the one who will love me with

the same intensity,
the same density,
the same fire,
the same desire,
the same emotion,
the same deep-as-any-ocean love
that I promise to have for him.

Nia

Nia is a Swahili word.
Purpose is what it means.
My own unique purpose I continually seek,
as I strive to give substance to my dreams.

My purpose is not to contaminate my body
with alcohol, cigarettes, or dope.
My purpose is to strive for success,
to seek encouragement and not lose hope.

My purpose is not to contaminate my mind
or fill it with vileness and corruption,
but to seek after knowledge and after truth,
shunning paths that lead to destruction.

My purpose is not to corrupt my spirit
or feel inadequate next to any man (or woman),
but to know that I am uniquely wonderful and talented,
for I was formed with the Almighty's hand.

The harmony of my body, mind, and spirit
are the cause of my self-esteem high.
And I can reach any goal I set for myself,
my only limit is the unending sky.

On Marriage

As I read the Bible, Ephesians Five,
I get the distinct impression
that the main reason for the high divorce rate
is betrayal and sexual indiscretion,

Because many a spouses' shining eyes
have had cause to well up with tears
because of their beloved's misplaced affections
causing their sobs to fall on deaf ears.

The wife is compared to the church,
with Jesus in the husband's place.
Oh, the sacrifices that He made
for His church to reserve heaven's space.

It was for His church that He shed His blood.
So much that He gave His own life
to Hell and back He went, took the sting out of death.
Would today's husband do this for his wife?

If a husband is willing to truly accept
the pleasant yoke of marital bliss,
he must be aware of the depth of love
upon which his bride should always insist.

And the wife should present herself spotless
in her mind and heart, only pure thoughts
to be worthy of the showers of love
that flow from her husband's heart.

For what wise and godly woman
would not be steadfast at the side of one
who loves her as completely?
And to him, her equal, there is none..

For less than this brings great pain,
And eventually what comes to pass
is emotional tribulation, broken hearts once whole
resulting from promises made too fast.

For the godly marriage is sacred,
and the promises made are true,
and as the couple travels life's road together,
each day their vows are renewed.

Parenting

Parents, don't you know that we kids
are watching all the things you do.
And when you tell us to do this and not that,
sometimes your message just won't come through.

For if you tell us this and then do that,
your words won't have much power
to influence us kids not to do the very things
that cause sorrows on us to shower.

So parents, beware of our tender ears
to which you continually preach,
because they can fill up with wax and not benefit from
the good lessons that you try to teach.

Please Don't . . .

Please don't spend the rest of your life
proving that your elders were right,
doing all the things they told you to shun
and getting into plight after plight.

Please don't spend the rest of your life
proving that your parents weren't lying
by falling into pitfalls that they warned you about,
guaranteed to result in pain and sighing.

Please don't spend the rest of your life
proving that the Bible is true,
thinking that you'll be the one to escape
and no one will find out wrongs you do.

Instead, take heed of responsible warnings.
Benefit from the knowledge of how
to keep from falling into the same old holes
that existed then and still exist now.

So stop, listen, analyze, and learn.
Let wisdom and knowledge guide your actions
so that little time will be spent correcting unnecessary mistakes
and life will bring more satisfaction.

Procrastination

There's always a reason
not to do what you should.
There's always a detail
deliberately misunderstood.

There's always an excuse
for the tasks left undone:
"It was too hard," or
"I was having so much fun"

"I must have forgotten," or
"Tomorrow, I will do it."
"I really don't know how," or
"There's no time to get through it."

Eventually, sooner or later,
we all reap just what we sow.
But seeds left unplanted
will surely never grow.

Purpose

From the moment we are born,
we struggle and strive to know
the purpose our lives must fulfill,
the direction our feet should go.

As little children, we know to continually seek
the individual reason for our lives,
asking questions from dusk to dawn
to discover the mystery, we strive.

Though we are each individuals,
we'll need to give and receive affection.
And we need to be loved and cared for,
but so often we're wounded by rejection.

For love is such a basic need.
many become reckless in their pursuit,
and then love dies quickly like cut flowers,
for cut flowers have no root.

For God is the one true author of love,
and only from His example can we learn
that it's His love that makes us whole
so our own self-love can be earned.

So my message to you is quite simple:
Know that true love can only be found
once you acknowledge He that loved you first,
and His love in you abounds.

Sandcastles

A child will spend all day
building a castle in the sand,
deeply intent on its every detail,
making the sand bow to his command.

The windows must be identical.
Its many steeples must be so tall.
The courtyards must be magnificent
and fit for the grandest ball.

Bright seashells serve as awnings,
and when the sun shines on them just right,
rainbows seem to hover around,
displaying beautiful, pastel-colored light.

But alas, the tide, it must come in,
and in haste a child may forget
that the waves will put an end to the work
that a wall is needed to protect.

When the tide has done the deed
and tears make it hard to see,
I am reminded of a revelation
that God has shown to me.

He showed me how important
it is first to Him to pray
and to ask that He bless our endeavors
so the "thief" cannot take them away.

For the "thief" is mad with rage
and wishes to destroy us all.
Our hopes, our dreams, and all our blessings
are not safe without God's wall.

Sister, Sister

Sister, sister of my dreams,
do you exist, or am I being too extreme?

You're the one who doesn't curse
or have a mouth like a gutter.
You're the one who doesn't do
one boy after the other.

You're the one with standards.
Can't be bought with any price:
Even if the wallet's fat,
even if the care is real nice.

You're the one who dresses neatly,
not like a freak or whore
who leads us guys to thinking that
you're just another easy score.

You're the one who is smart
and sets positive goals.
And as you implement your future plans,
success surely for you will unfold.

This is why I have no fear
of entrusting my heart to you.
And on a strong foundation, we can build our love
into one that's strong and true.

So You Say

So you say you love me
now more than any love you ever gave,
while with each and every drink you take,
another rock you throw on your grave.

So you say that you'll be with me
as long as you possibly can,
but with that blunt you're carrying,
with Mr. Death you strive to stand.

So you say that you'll love me forever,
but you keep shortening forever when
you keep puffing on those cigarettes
again and again and again.

I know we don't have knowledge of
the exact moment when we will die,
but it upsets me when you do things
that show you don't even try

To stay with me in this earth realm
as long as you possibly can.
Please! Put away all those vices
so I won't believe what you say is a sham.

Special

I am *so* special
that when my mother gave birth,
the angels sang and rejoiced
for her precious gift to the earth.

I am *so* wonderful
that when I started to grow,
the dark clouds allowed
their silver linings to show.

I am *so* magnificent
that when I spoke my first word,
the wind told the rain
it was the sweetest sound ever heard.

I am *so* beautiful
that wherever I go,
God's sun shines upon me
with its golden glow.

I am *all* of these things
and so very much more.
I am but one of the flowers
that He created earth for.

For we are *all* God's flowers,
so beautiful and so unique,
planted by Him in His garden,
Where we can hear His voice as He speaks,

Saying, "My love for you is endless,
and if you love Me, too,
you will treat others as yourself
because I love *them*, too."

Spoon People

Spoon people, spoon people,
always stirring up trouble.
The world would improve greatly.
Peace on earth would double

If somehow their mouths and lips
would just fall right off their face
and put an end to the gossip
that runs rampant in this place.

But since God loves spoon people
and the sun shines on them, too,
then we also must love spoon people,
but we can despise the things they do.

Stop the Madness

Brothers and sisters of Washington, D.C.
I just want to extend my hand
in friendship, not in adversity,
before we vanish off the face of this land.

We're the fastest dying people in the U.S.A.
Dying by the hand of our own kind.
We've got to stop this killing and come back to our senses,
and stop acting like we've lost our minds.

We've got to start respecting ourselves
so that we can start respecting each other.
Stop all the killing to settle petty disputes
and stop hatin' on your sisters and brothers.

We've got to stop all this killing!
We've got to stop this genocide!
We've got to stop all this hatred!
Too many mommas have already cried!

The Dentist

Whenever a boy comes up to you
and offers to give you his body,
make sure your eyes are open wide
and your hearing is sharp, not shoddy.

He says, "Baby, I can make you feel real good.
Make you forget from where you came.
Just give me a chance to thrill you,
and I'll make you forget your own name.

Or maybe we'll make a baby,
that is if I can knock you up.
Because condoms aren't guaranteed, you know,
and I've been known to make them bust.

You see, sleeping with me is no honor.
I just want my thrill and that's all.
I'll tell you whatever lie you wanna hear
to make you wanna gimme them drawers.

If you get pregnant, I'll even go as far as
to let you have the baby all by yourself.
And when you need help, either emotional or financial,
You'd BETTER look at somebody else!

I won't be there to help you pay
for your medicine when your health starts to fade.
I won't be there to hold your hand either
as you lie alone, dying from AIDS.

I'll probably be still spreading diseases
if I'm not dead already myself.
I only care about living for the moment,
and I SURE don't care about your health!

So, if you are ever honored with my presence
and I choose to stand close by your side,
just put yourself in the hands of "The Dentist,"
and just relax and open wide."

The Gift

When I was born, God sent me
to earth with a gift of love
to give to someone dear to me,
like a heavenly shower from above.

I gave the gift to my mother,
but she died and went away.
I gave my love to my father,
but after Mommy died, he didn't stay.

I tried to give it to my grandma
and to my aunt and my mom's best friend,
but they already had kids of their own,
and I just wasn't as special to them.

Then, I tried to give love to a boyfriend.
That seemed to work for a while,
until I caught him cheating on me
with that girl with the pretty smile.

Then another, and another, and another boyfriend,
seemed like I was going round and round.
I just wanted a safe place to put
my love so it would be safe and sound.

I got so tired of that old routine
that I decided to switch, still again.
And instead of giving my love to a boy,
I tried giving love to his girlfriend.

Well, that didn't work out either.
Our love couldn't have been really true.
She thought she wasn't being unfaithful to me
when she called another boy her "boo."

So, I got tired of all that heartache.
I got tired of giving my love in vain.
So, I finally just decided to stop
and let God take away my pain.

In His love, I found security.
In His hands, my heart was finally safe.
In Him, I could give love completely.
No chance of being left alone at the gate.

For God's love is forever,
and God's love is so complete
that my heart can rejoice in it always,
and my heart now is finally free.

The Nerve of You

What….What did you ask me?
I know you didn't expect me to say "yes."
How could you even make your mouth say the words?
I want no part of that mess!

Oh, K, know that you're not trippin'!
Don't even play like you're upset.
My mother has done more for me than you,
and I give her great respect.

But sometimes even when she asks me
to go where I don't want to go,
in spite of the love I have for her,
the answer is an emphatic NO!

So, I don't know where you got the notion
that you and me were like that.
You'd better do a reality check
before I tell you where you're really at!

If you ever want me to speak to you again,
I strongly suggest you never repeat
those same words to me in any order,
or I'll turn you into dead meat!

The New, No-Limit Soldier

The KKK has retired its sheets.
They lay folded neatly in their special holder.
The new instrument of terror is not a thing anymore.
It's the new, no-limit soldier.

The new, no-limit soldier is black,
specially trained to attack his own kind.
Abusing, womanizing, stealing, and killing
are continually what's on his mind.

The new, no-limit soldier loves his lifestyle
and doesn't know that he hates himself.
He thrives on the many lives he's able to destroy.
That's how he gains all his wealth.

Gunslingers, hit men, pimps, and drug dealers;
Of teachers and preachers, he takes no instruction.
He steals, lies, cheats, and kills until he embraces his own self-destruc-
tion.

The new, no-limit soldier is a victim.
But he seldom goes out alone.
He takes as many as he can with him
to a place called Hell, that's his home.

The Path You Choose

Young man standing on the corner,
selling his illegal treats
out in the open for all to observe
his freedom in grave jeopardy.

Young girl, dancing her heart out,
she's almost completely nude.
Lap dances, getting laid, and getting paid,
she doesn't care that she's being abused.

Little boy on a distant shore,
staring wistfully at the sea.
Tattered clothes; shoeless, blistered toes,
not knowing when he'll be able to eat.

Daydreaming about how wonderful
it would be to live in the U.S.A.,
where children get to be children
and spend time engaged in play

And get to pursue an education
to learn that one plus one equals two,
to become a doctor, lawyer, or dentist,
or whatever he wants to do.

So sad that a young man will spend
the rest of his life in jail
for selling illegal wares on the streets,
making his life a living hell.

Young girl, crying her heart out,
while a pimp anticipates some fun
as he prepares to break in another whore,
assembling the train that on her will run.

He didn't have to choose the road
that lead to the destruction of his life.
Other choices were there for him,
other choices that don't end in strife.

She didn't have to choose the road—
There were others that lead to wealth
without sacrificing self-respect or her body,
without sacrificing her health.

Wake up, you young citizens
Of these fifty united states!
Take a look at the consequences!
Take a look at the choices you make!

You can choose to be an entrepreneur.
You can choose to have good success.
You can choose to go to college,
and you are free to prepare for the test.

So, youth of America, WAKE UP
if your eyes don't already see
That success is well within your grasp
and only YOU hold the key.

The Prayer

Dear Heavenly Father, please, please be there.
You promised that You would; You promised that You'd care.

Let me paint You a picture, Lord, of this terrible, terrible scene.
I'm two and a half months pregnant, and I'm only fifteen.

I know that many times I have broken Your heart.
I knew it was a sin; I knew it from the start.

I didn't really love him more than I love You.
It's just that everybody's doing it, and I just wanted to be cool.

I'm not at all ready to become anyone's mother.
I just wanted to have fun and so did my lover.

A little baby would only steal my high school pleasure.
And all my carefree days would become pastime treasures.

I think I have decided what steps I will take
to correct this wrong and to right this mistake.

Now, this baby that's inside me, I just have to know.
Is it really alive yet? Cause I haven't yet begun to show.

I already know the answer; I already know the truth.
But it means not being a kid anymore; it means the end of my youth.

But I know down in my heart and soul, two wrongs don't make a right.
So, I've decided this child I'm carrying will someday see the light.

So, please, God, I implore you to never leave me and show me the way
to go on from here, because I'm so, so afraid.

Amen.

The Prom

Daddy, I am finally here,
here at my senior prom.
It seemed like today would never come.
Time seemed to take too long.

I love my dress; it's so classy,
a bold mixture of fuchsia and pink.
No, Dad, I didn't forget
that you told me not to drink.

I'm dancing now with my date.
Now, I'm chatting with some friends.
This night is really a dream come true,
and I wish it would never end.

Now the prom is over,
and I'm leaving with my ride.
I'm so happy and proud of myself, Daddy,
because no alcohol did I imbibe.

We're in the car now, Daddy.
I thought on my way home,
but in less time than it takes to blink,
a drunk driver into our lane did roam.

I tried to do what you said, Daddy,
so that I could get home safe,
but no one told that drunk driver
about the accident he was about to make.

I'm really scared now, Daddy.
Red blood is all on my pretty, pink dress.
Things seem to be getting darker now,
as blood begins to fill my chest.

Daddy, I think that I'm dying.
I wish I could see you once more.
I feel like I'm not going to make it.
I feel like my body's at war.

You had so many plans for me, Daddy.
I was supposed to go to college next year.
I really wanted to make you proud,
and at my graduation, hear you cheer.

I'll never be a mother, Daddy.
I'll never be anyone's wife.
It just doesn't seem fair, Daddy.
That a drunk driver has stolen my life.

The Real Thug

I had a talk with a real thug today.
It was a one-way conversation all the way.

I asked him why did he join that gang.
He said nothing, no, not one single thang.

I asked him why he had hurt so many.
His answer was silence; he didn't have any.

I asked him why his dear mother was dying.
The only answer I got was the cold wind sighing.

I asked him how I should raise his young son.
Even then he had no words, no, not even one.

Frustrated and hurt, I slowly turned around,
but not before blowing a kiss to the cold, cold ground.

The Solution

Look at the trees,
as the new leaves appear.
Look at the flowers,
products of the clouds' tears.

Look at the sun.
It rises every day.
And it never forgets
the path it must take.

Look at the stars,
twinkling so bright,
complimenting the moon
with extraordinary light.

All of these gifts
God to us gives
to remind us
that He still lives.

And everything that
we try to do
only comes to pass
when He sees it through.

So, lift up your head
and your eyes to the sky
when burdens get too heavy
and cause you to cry.

Remember who's in control
and who really holds the key
to tear down all the walls
that seem to imprison you and me.

For blessings are to be hoped
faithfully by we who pray,
and God makes it happen
and He's moving every day.

There's Loose Nerve Endings in the Classroom

There's loose nerve endings in the classroom.
Bumpin', thumpin', and turnin' around
like they've got an itch or something.
Seems like they just can't settle down.

In my classroom, they keep a comin'.
Anything but anxious to learn,
but I keep trying to enlighten them,
try to teach them how to discern.

But they just keep on actin' up
like their souls are on fire.
Thoughts of corruption and destruction,
of these, they never tire.

They should be more serious,
get good grades, follow the rules
so success can surely be theirs,
and stop calling me a fool!

I did the very things I teach them.
Why can't these children see
that if they do what I did,
they'd be as successful as me?

      I pay my bills late.
      I eat chicken, not steak.
      I feel my back against a rock.
      I keep trying to find a way
      to reach a brighter day.
      Seems no matter how hard I try,
      I'm just barely getting by.

Do you think that just perhaps
these children suspect the truth?
Do they see what I know now
in the tender years of their youth?

There's loose nerve endings in the classroom,
as loose as nerve endings can be.
And there's one that's gone plain hog-wild,
and that loose nerve ending is ME!

This Poem Does Not Rhyme

This poem does not rhyme.

The chords of my life are in a state of discord.

Why am I here? Why do I yet live?

Then, I stand there, looking at my child.

I tremble violently just thinking of the life he will live.

Like me, he will be chained.
Like me, he will be beaten.
Like me, he will be deprived of dignity.
Like me, he will be forced to work and toil with the only reward as having to face endless days of the same weariness wherein one longs for the day when darkness covers one's eyes while they are yet open.

Then, I look at you, my child, and my spirit begins to sigh greatly.

I know deep down in my heart that one day, someday in the future, those who come after me will be free.

Free from chains.
Free from beatings.
Free to respect others and be respected.
Free to work and earn with dignified independence.
Free to raise a family without being sold apart.
Free to be what the Creator first intended me to be.

My child, my descendant yet unborn. I will never get to speak to you because of the great boundary of time that lies between us.

I promise you that I will not pass on without passing my spirit of survival to my young one and the burning desire for him to pass it on to his off-spring.

And then, when you are free, my beloved, my soul will truly rest.

To the Million Man March Pledgees

Did The Million Man March
only affect that one day?
Did all the wonderful pledges you promised
to nothing dissolve away?

I'm still raising your children alone
without the financial support I need,
and my cries of desperation to you sound
like distant echoes of my greed.

I still need you to stop making me
the target of your great anger
by scarring my mind and body
not like a lover, but a stranger.

I still need you to elevate my stature
from "my baby's mother" to "my wife"
so that our family's foundation can be the strong one
on which our children can build their life.

I still need you to care for me as a father
and not make me your sexual toy.
Please allow me to grow up to be a woman
without scars from loveless exploits.

I still need you to seek after knowledge
and pursue a legitimate profession
so the frustration of being unemployed
does not lead to blind acts of aggression.

I still need you to stop cursing
an' communicating with words profane,
for these words aren't worthy to come from your lips,
so full of mockery and disdain.

I still need you to seek our Creator
and seek to illuminate your soul
so your steps in life may be guided
by the great Spirit about whom we've been told.

I still need you to stop blaming
the white man for wrongs he's done
and using that as your only excuse
for the reason your race has not won.

I still want to be there when you need me.
I still wait for you to offer me your hand.
I'm still waiting for The Million Man March Pledgees
to step forward and take command.

To the Real Men

The Million Man March for certain males
was that very special key
that unlocked the minds of many
who decided real men they would be.

No more will they watch the women
as they struggle to be "Mom" and "Dad,"
trying to provide for the little ones,
teaching them to choose good, not bad.

No longer will they watch as the women
alone struggle to pay all the debts.
No longer will her cries of frustration
ignored in a corner be swept.

For now is the time for real men
to step forward and take a firm stand.
And to proudly walk the avenues of life
not just as a male, but as a man.

Twisted Love

How do I love thee?
Let me count the ways.
I love you right now
and even to the end of your days.

As I stand at the bus stop
where you and I wait,
your visage is so appealing
that I'm totally snared by your bait.

Your shirt is so nice,
allowing much cleavage to show.
And your hip-hugging pants
tease my eyes, they're so low.

How I'd love to run my fingers
along the side of your face,
show you a night on the town,
take you all over the place.

But I know in my heart
that you won't give me a chance
to transform my fantasy
into a real romance.

It's just not fair
for you to taunt me like that.
Well, I'm not gonna take this.
Guess I'll have to change my hat.

So, I'll watch you and stalk you,
you won't even know
about the anger you caused in me
with your little skin show.

Soon you'll be begging me
when I make my move.
You won't have a choice
but to fit in my groove.

I will beat you and torture you
and smile when you cry.
I'll enjoy every minute,
even wipe tears from your eyes.

And when I am finished,
you'll tease me no more,
and I'll hide your nude body
under my basement floor.

Then, I'll go to work
and wait at the bus stop again.
Then another girl like you
will become my new friend.

What I Want for My Daughter

I want for my daughter a real love,
a true love that will never die,
a love that will bring joy to her heart
and never make her cry.

I want for my daughter someone who
delights even in the sound of her voice,
who never tires of her companionship
so other women *never* become his choice.

I want for my daughter a real man
who is so confident in her love for him
that jealousy has no room in the relationship
and simply cannot enter in.

I want for my daughter a godly man
whose desire is to please God above
and to sit in the front row of the classroom
where the Teacher is the Author of Love.

For if he loves her in this manner,
I am confident their love will grow,
and my thoughts of my dear daughter
will bring peace unto my soul.

Yes, No

Peace…Yes
War…No
Organization…Yes
Confusion…NO
Happiness…Yes
Sadness…No
Love…Yes
Hate…No
Harmony…Yes
Discord…No
Abundance…Yes
Pestilence…No
Smiles…Yes
Frowns…No
Joy…Yes
Envy…No
Truth…Yes
Lies…No
Right…Yes
Wrong…No
Heaven…Yes
and HELL…NO!

DATE DUE

PRINTED IN U.S.A.